Women Pray

QUIN SHERRER
AND
RUTHANNE GARLOCK

KINGSWAY PUBLICATIONS
EASTBOURNE

First published in the USA by Vine Books,
an imprint of Servant Publications.

First British edition 2001

ISBN 0 85476 986 2

Published by
KINGSWAY PUBLICATIONS
Lottbridge Drove, Eastbourne, BN23 6NT, England.
Email: books@kingsway.co.uk

Book design and production for the publishers by
Bookprint Creative Services, P.O. Box 827, BN21 3YJ, England.
Printed in Great Britain.

Reproduced from the original text by arrangement with
Servant Publications.

dedicated to our

daughters and granddaughters

Quin's:

Quinett, Sherry, Dana

Kara, Evangeline, Victoria

Ruthanne's:

Linda, Melody

Amanda, Rachel, Lydia

Pray all the time.
Ask God for anything in line
with the Holy Spirit's wishes. Plead with him,
reminding him of your needs, and keep praying
earnestly for all Christians everywhere.

EPHESIANS 6:18 (TLB)

Contents

Introduction / 11

Part 1: ***Praying With Power***

I'm Too Busy Not to Pray / 14

Speak, Lord, I'm Listening / 14

Praying in Harmony with God's Will / 15

Teach Me How to Persist in Prayer / 15

Thank You for the Holy Spirit / 16

Finding Partners in Prayer / 17

Heed the Call to Fast and Pray / 17

My Most Important Prayer / 18

Scriptures for Power Praying / 19

Part 2: ***My Milestones and Special Occasions***

Engagement / 22

The Wedding / 22

I'm Pregnant / 23

My Firstborn / 23

Easter Celebration / 24

My Birthday / 25

My Nest Is Empty / 26

Thank You for My Job / 27

Now I'm a Grandmother! / 27

Our Christmas Gathering / 28

I Am Moving / 29

Home Again! / 29

My Health Report / 30

Recovering from Surgery / 30

Midlife Crisis / 31
My Husband's Death / 32
A Difficult Transition / 33
Death Is Near / 34
Scriptures for Meditation / 34

Part 3: *Praying for My Children*

Lord, Give Us Children / 38
For the Child in My Womb / 38
Thank You for My Newborn Child / 39
Protect My Children / 39
Guide Them in Your Way / 40
Equip Me to Love Them Unconditionally / 41
My Child Is Sick / 42
For My Newly Adopted Child / 43
For a Disabled Child / 44
For Stepchildren / 45
Protect My Children's Minds / 46
For My Children's Friends / 47
For My Children's Teachers / 47
My Child's Graduation / 48
My Child Needs a Job / 48
For My Children's Employers / 49
My Child Is Hurting / 49
When My Child Disappoints Me / 50
Deliver My Child from Addiction / 51
My Unmarried Daughter Is Pregnant / 52
My Unmarried Son Has Made a Girl Pregnant / 53
Prodigal Children / 54
Rejoicing over a Prodigal's Return / 55
For My Son's Future Wife / 56
My Son's Marriage / 57

For My Daughter's Future Husband / 58
My Daughter's Wedding Day / 59
My Child Is Getting a Divorce / 60
My Daughter Has Been Abused / 61
For My Grandchildren / 62
Scriptures to Pray for Children / 63

Part 4: *Praying for My Husband*

Thank You for Him / 66
Strengthen My Husband in Every Way / 66
Bless Him in All Areas of Life / 67
Improve Our Communication / 68
I Forgive Him / 69
Prayer for a Husband's Job / 69
Help Him Be a Good Father / 70
Gone Away for Awhile / 71
Help Me Not to Complain / 71
My Husband Doesn't Know You, Lord / 72
Help Him See the Light / 72
Restore Our Marriage / 73
He Wants a Divorce / 74
Scriptures for Meditation / 75

Part 5: *Praying for Family and Friends*

Guide Me in Praying for Others / 78
Loved Ones Who Are Lost / 79
Stormy Circumstances / 80
Tough Times for Our Family / 80
Away from Home / 81
Prayer for My Colleagues / 81

May I Love My Parents Well / 82
I Forgive My Parents / 83
My Parents Are Aging / 84
My Parents Don't Know You, Lord / 85
For Sins That Harass Our Family / 86
Bless Our Family and Home / 87
Healing of a Loved One / 88
Scriptures for Meditation / 89

Part 6: *Prayers Singles Pray*
Lord, I Need a Friend / 92
It's Not Easy Being Single / 92
Thank You for My Family / 93
Single Again / 93
A New Relationship / 94
Help Me Reach Out to Others / 95
Scriptures for Meditation / 96

Part 7: *Praying Through Tough Times*
Balancing Home and Work / 100
Help Me Get through the Day / 101
Sleep Escapes Me / 101
I Don't Understand, Lord / 102
My Cloud of Depression Is Lifting / 103
Nothing Is Impossible / 103
Walk Me through My Pain / 104
Falsely Accused / 105
You Are My Rock / 106
I'm So Disappointed, Lord / 107
I Lost a Child / 108

Exchanging Self-Pity for Hope / 109
My Friend Has Died / 110
My Husband Is Gone / 111
Scriptures for Meditation / 112

Part 8: *When I Am Afraid*
Lord, I Need a Job / 116
I Cast My Worry on You / 117
You Are My Refuge / 117
Victory over Fear / 118
Scriptures for Meditation / 119

Part 9: *Prayers of Thanksgiving and Praise*
Worthy of Worship / 122
Joining Heaven's Choir / 123
A Brand-New Year / 124
Thank You for Spring / 125
I Will Praise You, Regardless / 126
Thank You That Mourning Is Over / 127
Thanksgiving Prayer / 128
Scriptures for Praise and Worship / 129

Part 10: *Purify My Life*
I Complained Today / 134
Not My Will but Yours / 134
Shine Your Light into My Dark Corners / 135
Make Me Like You / 135
Clothe Me in Your Strength / 136
Wipe My Slate Clean / 136
Guilty No More / 137
When I Have Failed You, Lord / 137

Overcoming Sin / 138
Resisting Temptation / 138
Protect Me from the Evil One / 139
Thank You for the Holy Spirit / 139
Direct My Path / 140
My Spiritual Gifts / 140
Let Me Bear Fruit / 141
Scriptures for the Overcomer / 142

Part 11: *When I Need to Forgive*
I Am Angry, Lord / 146
Help Me Forgive Those Who Hurt Me / 147
Help Me Show Mercy / 148
I Am Forgiven / 148
I Want to Mend This Broken Relationship / 149
Scriptures for Meditation / 149

Part 12: *Praying for Neighbours, Community, and Leaders*
I Neglected My Neighbour / 152
Divine Appointments / 152
Help Me with Sandpaper People / 153
Prayer for My Pastor / 154
Prayer for Our Schools / 155
Prayer for the Justice System / 156
Prayer for Leaders / 157
Scriptures for Our Nation's Leaders / 157

Bibliography / 160

Introduction

Most women today live busy, crowded lives. Perhaps you think you don't have time to pray. We wrote this book with you in mind—to help you focus on things you'd like to talk to God about.

Prayer is the link between us and God. Our way of communicating with him. And our times of quiet meditation are the moments when God communicates with us. You could call it the "divine connection."

Actually—no matter how busy you are—nothing is more important than keeping that connection alive through prayer.

We invite you, through the pages of this book, to take time for intimate moments with God—whether you're in the midst of sorrow or of joy. These golden "time-bites" will help you set your sails to catch the wind, and keep you on an even keel, despite the storms of life.

The *form* of your prayer is not so important as the *fact* of your praying regularly to keep the "divine connection" viable. Formal language isn't necessary. But honesty is. Prayer is simply talking to God as you would talk to your best friend. Express your deepest feelings. Admit your mistakes. Ask for his help. Wait for his answer.

When Jesus lived on earth, he taught his followers what is known as "The Lord's Prayer." It is simply a guideline showing the elements our prayers should include:

- Giving adoration and praise to God
- Expressing concern beyond our own needs—that God's will be done throughout the earth
- Bringing to him our personal needs

- Asking for forgiveness
- Being willing to forgive others
- Asking for divine protection
- Acknowledging and declaring God's omnipotent power.

Jesus' Instructions on Prayer

"When you pray, go into your room, and when you have shut your door, pray to your Father who is in the secret place; and your Father who sees in secret will reward you openly.... Do not use vain repetitions as the heathen do. For they think that they will be heard for their many words. Therefore do not be like them. For your Father knows the things you have need of before you ask Him. In this manner, therefore, pray:

> "Our Father in heaven,
> Hallowed be Your name.
> Your kingdom come.
> Your will be done
> On earth as it is in heaven.
> Give us this day our daily bread.
> And forgive us our debts,
> As we forgive our debtors.
> And do not lead us into temptation,
> But deliver us from the evil one.
> For Yours is the kingdom and
> the power and the glory forever. Amen."

MATTHEW 6:6-13 (NKJ)

Our hope is that your relationship with God will grow in fervour and intimacy as you pray these prayers.

—Quin Sherrer and Ruthanne Garlock

Part One

Praying with Power

I'm Too Busy Not to Pray

Too busy to pray, I thought, Lord. I didn't stop to ask you what to do today. I plunged headlong into my own plans. I took too many detours. Slowing me down, frustrating me. How much I need to ask you first to order my day, direct my paths, and help me not to get sidetracked by my "must-get-done list." I missed our morning talk. Lord, forgive me. In Jesus' name, Amen.

Speak, Lord, I'm Listening

How to hear you, Lord? How I wish I knew how to quiet my heart sufficiently to hear your clear direction. A million voices cry out and I can't discern which one is yours. I'm sorry, so sorry. I didn't still my heart to hear your voice alone today.

I'll wait in silence now. Speak, Lord, I'm listening....

Praying in Harmony with God's Will

Lord, thank you that I can come fearlessly, boldly, confidently to you in prayer. Reveal to me things I need to know and understand—helping me to pray more effectively and to pray what is on your heart. Purify my heart so I will ask with the right motive, confident that you want to answer. Thank you for the privilege of prayer! I give you praise in Jesus' name, Amen.

Teach Me How to Persist in Prayer

Lord, I thank you that you have taught us to pray specifically and with persistence, assuring us that when we ask, you hear. When we knock, you open (Luke 11:5-13). Thank you for being such a loving, caring Father. Help me to be tenacious and faithful in prayer. But, Lord, forgive me when I expect you to answer according to my timetable and in my precise way. You know far more about my needs and concerns than I do. Help me to trust you during the waiting time. I ask in Jesus' name, Amen.

Thank You for the Holy Spirit

Lord, thank you for your incredible gift of the Holy Spirit, whom you sent to live within believers after Jesus left this earth. Thank you that when I don't know exactly how I ought to pray, the Spirit himself will intercede for me in accordance with God's will—if I will but ask him (Romans 8: 26-27).

I sit quietly waiting for the words to pray. Now let your Holy Spirit put thoughts in my mind which are aligned with your will regarding the situation I'm concerned about. Thank you, Lord, for the Holy Spirit—my Helper. I want to learn how to pray, as well as how to worship you more completely. Amen.

Finding Partners in Prayer

Father, show me whom you want me to pray with on a regular basis. Bring the name of that person to my mind. And also move on her heart if it is your plan for us to be a prayer team. I ask you to teach us how to pray in agreement with you.

Lord, I need a prayer support system. Please bring me into fellowship with a group of Christians willing to help carry my prayer burden. May I also be an encouragement to them. Thank you, Lord, for these special people you will bring across my path. Amen.

Heed the Call to Fast and Pray

Lord, give me your strength to fast and pray as I seek your direction. I know fasting can accomplish much in my own life and also in the situation for which I'm interceding (Matthew 6:16-18). Guide me as to how long to fast. My spirit is willing, but my body sometimes weakens. Give me your wisdom, Lord. Speak to me through your Word, and help me glorify you through my fasting. I thank you in Jesus' name, Amen.

My Most Important Prayer

Jesus, God's Son, came to earth and took the blame for the sin of our pride, rebellion, and selfishness which separated all mankind from God. Thus he closed the gap between us and God. When we confess our sin and receive his forgiveness, we then can freely approach God with our needs. Pray this prayer to make Jesus Lord of your life.

Lord Jesus, I confess that I've sinned against you. Please forgive me for walking in my own selfish ways, and wash me clean. I receive you as my Lord and Savior. I believe you are the Son of God, who came to earth, died on the cross, shed your blood for my sins, and arose from the dead. Give me your strength, Lord. Help me live my life to please you. Thank you for opening the way for me to pray to God the Father in your name. I rejoice in your promise that I will live with you forever in heaven. Amen.

Scriptures for Power Praying

In you I trust, O my God. Do not let me be put to shame, nor let my enemies triumph over me.

PSALM 25:2

"Is not this the kind of fasting I have chosen: to loose the chains of injustice and untie the cords of the yoke, to set the oppressed free and break every yoke?" ISAIAH 58:6

"I have given you authority to trample on snakes and scorpions and to overcome all the power of the enemy; nothing will harm you." LUKE 10:19

"I have told you these things, so that in me you may have peace. In this world you will have trouble. But take heart! I have overcome the world." JOHN 16:33

But thanks be to God! He gives us the victory through our Lord Jesus Christ.

1 CORINTHIANS 15:57

For though we live in the world, we do not wage war as the world does. The weapons we fight with are not the weapons of the world. On the contrary, they have divine power to demolish strongholds. We demolish arguments and every pretension that sets itself up against the knowledge of God, and we take captive every thought to make it obedient to Christ.

2 Corinthians 10:3-5

Be self-controlled and alert. Your enemy the devil prowls around like a roaring lion looking for someone to devour. 1 Peter 5:8

Submit yourselves, then, to God. Resist the devil, and he will flee from you. James 4:7

Finally, be strong in the Lord and in his mighty power. Put on the full armour of God so that you can take your stand against the devil's schemes. For our struggle is not against flesh and blood, but against the rulers, against the authorities, against the powers of this dark world and against the spiritual forces of evil in the heavenly realms. Therefore put on the full armour of God, so that when the day of evil comes, you may be able to stand your ground, and after you have done everything, to stand. Ephesians 6:10-13

Part Two

My Milestones and Special Occasions

Engagement

Lord, he wants me to spend the rest of my life with him. Imagine, he chose me! I'm excited about our future. But I admit I'm apprehensive too. Will I make a good wife? Lord, help me. Teach me. Send a mentor—a woman who has a successful marriage—who can give me godly advice. Lord, help us with planning our wedding. Then help us through the stress of so many adjustments. May I lean into you for guidance one day at a time. In Jesus' name, Amen.

The Wedding

Lord, I invite you to be a part of our wedding and to bless this milestone day in my life. May I radiate your inner beauty when I step into my wedding dress. I'm nervous, Lord. A busy time with so many friends and family to greet. Then to go away for a honeymoon with the one I love. Help me adapt to my new life, beginning on my wedding night! Teach me to be the wife I need to be for the special man you've given me. Thank you so much for him. Amen.

I'm Pregnant

I'm pregnant! Joy unspeakable. Lord, I give you thanks and praise for allowing me the awesome responsibility to be called "a mother." Prepare me for motherhood both physically and emotionally. Bless and protect the little one in my womb. Help me through nausea, sleepiness, and craving for silly foods. Encourage my husband and help him understand the adjustments I'm having to make because of my pregnancy. Lord, I'm trusting you for a safe delivery. Amen.

My Firstborn

Lord, thank you for this tiny bundle you put into my arms today. How precious is your gift of life! How beautiful! Give my husband and me wisdom to raise this child for your glory. So much lies ahead for both of us, but I am awed by this baby. So tiny. So vulnerable. So totally dependent on me. Make me a capable mother! Help me to follow your ways so my child will have a lifelong love and devotion for you, Lord. Amen.

Easter Celebration

How I love this marvellous season when we celebrate your resurrection. Thank you, Lord Jesus, for your willingness to die on the cross for our sins. And thank you for coming back from death to give us new life. I'm so sorry the world causes people to focus on bunnies, Easter eggs, and chocolates, instead of on you. Lord, help me instil in my children the miracle of your resurrection. I want to observe this special day in a way pleasing to you. In Jesus' name, Amen.

My Birthday

Thank you for another birthday—another year! Some people count wrinkles or grey hair. I count my blessings. Thank you for my health, my family, my friends, my home, my food and shelter. Lord, I never want to take these things for granted. Thank you for sustaining me through this past year. With every problem I faced, your wisdom faithfully guided me. Whenever I felt weak, I could lean on your strength. In the year ahead, please direct my path and help me reflect your love to all around me. You've been gracious to me. Thank you, Lord. Amen.

My Nest Is Empty

How I miss my children since they've all left the nest, Lord. It seems their years at home just evaporated. Now they're off to college or to distant jobs, and the house is strangely quiet. I find myself imagining what one of them may be doing at any given moment. When the phone rings, I hope it might be one of them calling home.

Thank you, Lord, that your eye is upon each of my children and that your protection continues to cover them. Prepare them for the future. Help them resist evil and be examples of godliness wherever they go. You know all about their mistakes, Lord. But how grateful I am that you can redeem the mistakes all of us have made! Help me fulfil your purpose for my life now that the nest is empty. In Jesus' name, Amen.

Thank You for My Job

Thank you, Lord, for a job where I can use my talents in a profession I enjoy. Help me to do my best work and to be an example of Christ's character to those with whom I interact. Thank you that my family encourages me to use my abilities and skills in the workplace. I'll never forget that you gave me these talents. Help me grow in wisdom, Lord, and protect me from allowing my job to take precedence over my relationship with you or with my family. I give you praise. Amen.

Now I'm a Grandmother!

I praise you, Lord, for the gift of my grandchildren. It's such a wonderful time of life to enjoy these children but not have to carry the full responsibility for them. Give their parents wisdom to nurture them in your ways, and guide me in how to pray for their future. May I be a good example and a fun companion for them. Make me sensitive to special needs they may have that I could help meet. Lord, I don't want to play favourites among my grandchildren. Give me your wisdom; I ask in Jesus' name, Amen.

Our Christmas Gathering

What a glorious time of year when we celebrate your birth! Although the world has greatly commercialized it, it's a special holiday that bears your name, Lord. Thank you for the opportunities you'll provide for me to reach out to my family, my friends, and others—to touch them with your love. I pray you will be present at our family gathering. Help me, by example, to teach my children and grandchildren the importance of honouring you on this special day. Lord, you know all about rifts and hard feelings between family members. I pray that when we gather, healing and reconciliation will come where it is needed. Thank you, Father, for sending us your Son at Christmastime. Amen.

I Am Moving

Lord, how hard it is for me to pack. I'm leaving behind my neighbours, my church family, and my dearest friends. Of course, right now I'm sad. I cry when a friend comes over to say goodbye. But I know you are in this move and you will give me new friends and a new church home. I can make this transition only by knowing you are guiding me and watching over my life. Make it a joyful experience for me, Lord. I thank you for the new adventure that lies ahead. Amen.

Home Again!

Home again! Holiday time was fun but tiring. We tried to pack too much activity into our time away. But, Lord, even in my weariness, I came back with a new appreciation for our home. I see it through new eyes. No longer will I focus on its deficits—such as needing new carpet and paint. Now I see it as a haven for our family. More than just a shelter—it's a sanctuary. A safe, special place where we can always laugh, love, play, and pray together. Thank you, Lord, for my time away. It's renewed my gratitude for what I have here at home. Amen.

My Health Report

Thank you, Lord, for the check-up I passed today. A few minor problems, yes. Some discipline will now be required on my part to exercise and to watch my diet. But, Lord, I was so afraid, when I went in, that I had a major medical problem. I realize my body truly is a temple of the Holy Spirit, and I want to be a good steward of the temple you've given me. Help me to co-operate with you in getting my body in better shape. Thank you, Lord. Amen.

Recovering from Surgery

I had no idea, Lord, that it would take so long to recover from surgery. I'm weak. I've been such an independent woman. You know that. So help me to accept help without feeling resentful. I know only you can see me through this time when I feel so vulnerable, fragile, and unlovable. Please help my body recover quickly, with no complications. Thank you, Lord, for loving me and infusing me with your strength. Amen.

A Difficult Transition

Lord, I don't want to make this move. I don't feel like it—physically or emotionally. It's hard to think about leaving behind most of my lifelong belongings and my close neighbours to move into a retirement home. I'm scared. Confused. Actually unwilling to move. Lord, show me some positive things that will come from this transition. Change my attitude. Have your way with me in my new surroundings. I yield to your plan for me, even in these waning years of my life. Help me to be your woman of grace and dignity. In Jesus' name, Amen.

Death Is Near

I feel it in my spirit. Lord, it won't be long before my life on earth is over. Prepare me and prepare my children for that day. My departure will be painful for them but glorious for me. My old body is wearing out. I'm ready to go. How much easier it is for me, because I know Jesus has gone ahead and prepared a place for me in heaven. Help my family accept my passing into new life with you as just another milestone. May they be better prepared for their own death as they watch me cling to you in my last days. Give me peace as I slip into your presence. Precious Lord … hold my hand. Amen.

Scriptures for Meditation

Do you not know that your body is a temple of the Holy Spirit, who is in you, whom you have received from God? You are not your own; you were bought at a price. Therefore honour God with your body. 1 CORINTHIANS 6:19-20

It is God who is at work in [me], both to will and to work for His good pleasure.

PHILIPPIANS 2:13 (NASB)

Be content with what you have, because God has said, "Never will I leave you; never will I forsake you."

HEBREWS 13:5

The Lord is my shepherd, I shall not be in want. He makes me lie down in green pastures, he leads me beside quiet waters, he restores my soul. He guides me in paths of righteousness for his name's sake. Even though I walk through the valley of the shadow of death, I will fear no evil, for you are with me; your rod and your staff, they comfort me. You prepare a table before me in the presence of my enemies. You anoint my head with oil; my cup overflows. Surely goodness and love will follow me all the days of my life, and I will dwell in the house of the Lord forever.

PSALM 23:1-6

If I say, "Surely the darkness will hide me and the light become night around me," even the darkness will not be dark to you; the night will shine like the day, for darkness is as light to you. For you created my inmost being; you knit me together in my mother's womb. I praise you because I am fearfully and wonderfully made; your works are wonderful, I know that full well. My frame was not hidden from you when I was made in the secret place. When I was woven together in the depths of the earth, your eyes saw my unformed body. All the days ordained for me were written in your book before one of them came to be. How precious to me are your thoughts, O God! How vast is the sum of them! Were I to count them, they would outnumber the grains of sand. When I awake, I am still with you.

PSALM 139:11-18

In my Father's house are many rooms; if it were not so, I would have told you. I am going there to prepare a place for you. JOHN 14:2

Lord, you have been our dwelling place throughout all generations.... Teach us to number our days aright, that we may gain a heart of wisdom.

PSALM 90:1, 12

Part Three

Praying for My Children

Lord, Give Us Children

Heavenly Father, you see our empty cradle, and you see our great desire to have children. Your Word confirms that you truly are a Father to us, and we know you have a special love for children. Lord, we pray you will answer our hearts' cry for a child, whether by birth or by adoption. But we submit our wills to you and trust your great plan and purpose for our lives. Please, Lord, cause your presence and your peace to sustain us as we wait upon you. In Jesus' name, Amen.

For the Child in My Womb

Lord, I pray for the child I am carrying in my womb. Even from this early stage, may this baby feel my love and acceptance. Oh, the dreams and plans I have for him or her! But, Lord, help me be willing to lay them aside for your greater purposes. I'm trusting you, Lord, to help me carry this child full-term and have a safe delivery. Be with all the doctors and nurses who will be attending me. Give them wisdom beyond their experience during the birth of my baby. Thank you, Lord, for giving life! Amen.

Thank You for My Newborn Child

Lord, how I praise you for this new life you've entrusted to me. My child is fearfully and wonderfully made. Children are a reward from you, so I thank you for this blessing. Help me to wisely nurture my child. May this dear baby grow in wisdom and stature and favour with God and man, as Jesus did. Please protect and direct his/her steps, and may my child's life bring honour and glory to you. I pray in Jesus' name, Amen.

Protect My Children

Father God, creator of all things, I thank you for the gift of my children. I ask you to dispatch angels to watch over them and protect them in all their ways (Psalm 91:11). Send Christian friends into their lives to help them and to be godly influences. Lord, what an awesome privilege and responsibility to be a parent. Help me discern when my children need my special prayers or my help. Give me wisdom to be the parent I need to be, and help me to be an understanding friend to ________________ *(name or names)*. Thank you, Lord. Amen.

Guide Them in Your Way

Father, may my children fulfil your plan and purpose for their lives. May the Spirit of the Lord be upon them ... "the Spirit of wisdom and of understanding, the Spirit of counsel and of power, the Spirit of knowledge and of the fear of the Lord ..."(Isaiah 11:2). Lord, I release my children into your hands. Thank you that you love them more than I do, that your plans for them are plans for welfare and peace, not for evil, and that you will give them a future of hope (Jeremiah 29:11). Amen.

Equip Me to Love Them Unconditionally

Thank you, Lord, for loving us unconditionally and for helping us do the same for our children. Father, may I, like you, be a perpetual forgiver. I admit that when my children try my patience, they are not easy to love with my own human love. At those times, equip me to love them with your love (Romans 5:5).

Help us show our children what precious gifts they are to us and how much we love, appreciate, and treasure them. Guide us in ways we can be better parents. In Jesus' name, I ask, Amen.

My Child Is Sick

Dear Jesus, I know you cared enough about little children when you walked the earth to touch them, to heal them. My child is sick and needs your soothing touch. Lord, we ask for the right doctor, the right hospital, and the right treatment. Most of all we need you, The Great Physician. Give us wisdom to make right choices. Give the medical people wisdom in treatment. Lord, I know you can heal instantly if you choose. I cry out on behalf of my child. Please heal this disease. Thank you. Amen.

For My Newly Adopted Child

Heavenly Father, thank you for the opportunity you have given me to rear this precious child, this wonderful gift. May you show me how to love and care for __________ so that he/she will grow up to know and honour you. Bless his/her life with your love and peace. Help me be an excellent mother; may this child never feel rejected or abandoned. Lord, I thank you for the birth parents who brought __________ into the world, and I ask your blessing upon them as well. I consecrate this child to you. In Jesus' name, Amen.

For a Disabled Child

God, thank you for trusting me to care for this special child you have brought into our family. Help me never to forget it is a privilege to care for this dear one. I trust you to make this child a blessing, regardless of his/her limitations. I know you have a plan for ________, just as you do for our other children. When I grow discouraged, give me your unconditional love to pour into this child and strength and wisdom to meet those special needs. Thank you for supplying it, Lord. In Jesus' name, Amen.

For Stepchildren

Lord, show me creative ways to express your love and mine to my stepchildren. You know I sometimes become angry with them. But I need to see each of my children and stepchildren as you see them. Help me to be more loving and understanding. Show me when to speak and when to be quiet. When to discipline and when to be more lenient. Help us to be honest enough to communicate freely, without hurting one another.

Thank you for my stepchildren's good qualities, Lord, and for all the potential in their lives. I ask you to heal their hurts and disappointments. Lord, bless the parent they are separated from. May Jesus be Lord of all our lives. In his name I pray, Amen.

Protect My Children's Minds

Lord, protect my children's minds. Help me direct their learning in the proper ways. How easy it is for the world's views—so contrary to your ways—to creep into their minds through toys, television, games, books, videos, friends, and teachers. Give them wisdom to choose your better way. Help them filter out the ungodly and untrue philosophies that daily bombard them.

Give my children, as you did Daniel, "knowledge and understanding of all kinds of literature and learning." Help my children understand the times in which they live and provide them with strength and wisdom to serve you in these times (Daniel 1:17, 20). Thank you in Jesus' name, Amen.

For My Children's Friends

Thank you, Lord, for my children's friends. May they be a blessing to one another. I continue to pray for the right friends to come into my children's lives at the right time. Because your Word says bad company corrupts morals, I ask that you guard them from wrong friendships and wrong influences. Help them to be strong in you, Lord. Amen.

For My Children's Teachers

Lord, you told us to pray for those in authority over us. My children have many teachers in authority over them, and I ask you to bless each one. Reveal your love to them, and meet their needs. Cause them to have godly wisdom to impart to my children. Keep them from leading their pupils astray with ideas contrary to your Word. I ask you to direct my children to the teachers and role models from whom they can best learn and prepare for the future. Thank you for each one of these teachers, Lord. Amen.

My Child's Graduation

Commencement! A new beginning. Thank you, Lord, for this great day. With all the congratulations being extended, I can't let Graduation Day pass without acknowledging your help in getting my child to this point. Be with __________ during the ceremonies today. We are so proud of our child for perseverance in reaching this goal. Protect him/her from danger during celebrations tonight. Continue to direct his/her future choices and plans. College. Career. Marriage. Thank you, Lord, that we can trust you for all of these! Amen.

My Child Needs a Job

Lord, my child has searched and searched for the right job, without success. Please open a door of opportunity soon. Show him/her how to get through the application process, and provide favour when the interview takes place. Match ________'s talents with the company that needs his/her skills. Then help my child reflect your love in the workplace. Thank you, Lord, for your provision. I know nothing is impossible for you. Amen.

For My Children's Employers

I am so grateful, God, for those who employ my children in the workplace. Jobs enable them to use their talents in work that provides remuneration and gives them satisfaction in doing something they enjoy. Bless their employers, and may my children continue to find favour with them and with you. Give them sensitivity to know how to deal with a boss who's having a bad day. Give them creativity in performing their tasks. Help them shine for you wherever they go. Thank you for your blessings, Lord. Amen.

My Child Is Hurting

Lord, my child is wounded. Hurting so. I stand by helplessly, unable to alleviate ______'s pain and disappointment. Only you can bring healing. Let your soothing balm be poured over all the emotional bruises this event has caused. Heal ______'s broken heart and the memories associated with it. Help me to speak encouragement, blessing, and hope into my child's life and to love him/her unconditionally. I ask in Jesus' name, Amen.

When My Child Disappoints Me

Lord, I admit there are times when I am so disappointed in _______ that I can't see anything good or positive in him/her. Forgive me for only looking at the imperfections, forgetting that I need to trust you, who does everything in the right way and at the right time. Lord, only you know the deepest needs of my child's heart. Only you know when _______'s particular situation is fully ripe for your answer. Help me to make times of disappointment and heartache times of waiting in your presence for future usefulness. I commit ________ into your hands, Father, and I thank you that victory is on the way for this child whom you've given to us. In Jesus' name I pray, with thanksgiving for all your blessings. Amen.

Deliver My Child from Addiction

Lord, I praise you for being the Great Deliverer. I ask you to move mightily on behalf of our son/daughter, ______. Deliver him/her from evil. Show him/her a way of escape. Convict him/her of this destructive sin that prevents him/her from receiving your love. Father, thank you for the promise in your Word that "the seed of the righteous shall be delivered" (Proverbs 11:21, KJV). I am righteous because of the blood of Jesus, and ______ is my seed. So, Lord, I'm trusting you to deliver him/her from this trap and establish his/her life in your perfect plan. Thank you that what the enemy means for evil, you can turn to good (Genesis 50:20). I give you praise in Jesus' name, Amen.

My Unmarried Daughter Is Pregnant

Lord, I am so disappointed that ________ is pregnant. Even angry that her disobedience caused this dilemma. Help me to forgive her for having sex outside of marriage. I acknowledge that it was a sin, and I ask you to forgive both of them and to bring healing for this heartache. Father, you are the giver of life. Please protect ________ and the child in her womb. Give her your comfort and reveal your love to her.

Thank you, Lord, for forgiving me and my children for the times we have failed one another and for the times we have failed you. Help us to walk in forgiveness when others don't understand what we are going through. Lord, heal the broken relationships in our family and make something beautiful out of this ordeal. Give us your wisdom for the decisions we must make. Father, in Jesus' name we call upon you for mercy and strength in our time of need. Amen.

My Unmarried Son Has Made a Girl Pregnant

Lord, I must confess I'm angry because ________ has made his girlfriend pregnant. I beg your forgiveness for their foolish behaviour; help me also to forgive them, Lord. Give them wisdom as to what to do, especially in light of the baby's future. Should they marry? Or allow the baby to be adopted? My cry is that they will not choose abortion but allow this baby to live.

Lord, I feel such regret over their sin, yet I acknowledge that you are the giver of life. I pray for the child in the womb, that he or she will fulfil your purpose. Protect him or her from feelings of rejection. Bless the young mother of my grandbaby I may never even know. Help me show your love towards her and towards my son. I ask in Jesus' name, Amen.

Prodigal Children

Lord, may our prodigal children "come to their senses and escape from the trap of the devil" (2 Timothy 2:26)—just as the Prodigal Son did in the parable Jesus told. Lord, we anticipate the day when, through prayer and faith, our prodigals will turn their hearts towards you. We praise you for what you are doing in their hearts even now to draw them to Jesus. Give us your divine love for our children—even the rebellious, wayward ones. Help us to see them as you see them and to communicate more clearly with them. We stand on your Word that *nothing* is impossible with you. In Jesus' name, Amen.

Rejoicing over a Prodigal's Return

Thank you, Lord, for the prodigal child who has come home—to us and to you. How we praise you for this breakthrough, for this answer to prayer. We continue to believe your promises to us that our other children will return also.

I claim the promise that you will contend with those who contend with me, and you will save my children (Isaiah 49:25). Thank you that you will bring back from the land of the enemy those who have strayed (Jeremiah 31:16). I rejoice in your promises to me that your purposes will be fulfilled in their lives. Thank you for the gift of these precious children. Give me strength to continue to stand in the gap in prayer for them. In Jesus' name, Amen.

For My Son's Future Wife

Father God, send the Holy Spirit to bring my son's future wife to him. May she have the attributes for a godly wife and mother. I thank you in advance that she will be a jewel like the virtuous wife of Proverbs 31. May they both love and serve the Lord Jesus all their days. Lord, I pray that when this special young woman comes into ______________'s life, he will know it and be led by you for the timing of their marriage. Thank you for showing me how to pray for them in the future. Amen.

My Son's Marriage

Lord, he's getting married. Thank you that he found her! My heart swells with joy over his anticipation of starting his own home. Lord, from the beginning you said a man should leave his father and mother and cling only to his wife (Genesis 2:24). As his mother I release him—this fine young man you entrusted to our family. Help me love this young woman as my own daughter.

I pray you will be present at their wedding and that all who come will sense it. And as they start their own home, may you have first place there. When the storms of life come, may they anchor their faith in you. Lord, bless their union. In Jesus' name, Amen.

For My Daughter's Future Husband

Lord, you see my daughter's great desire to marry. I ask you to bring ______'s husband across her path in your perfect timing, and help her to be content until he comes. Protect my daughter from marrying outside your will. May her husband love the Lord with all his heart and embrace Jesus as his personal Saviour.

Thank you, Lord, that ______'s talents and gifts now being used in your kingdom's work will complement the talents of the one you are preparing for her. I pronounce a blessing upon them and thank you in advance for what you have planned for their future. Thank you for my future son-in-law. Bless him wherever he is. Amen.

My Daughter's Wedding Day

It's her wedding day, Lord. With your help, I've prepared her as best I can, and now I release her from our home to her husband. She's a beautiful bride, but, Lord, I thank you for the inner beauty that shines through her because she knows you. Right now she's probably got butterflies, or maybe even doubts. Quiet her spirit. Give her your peace. Help her enjoy this day.

Thank you for giving her to us for these short years. Now give her wisdom to be the wife and mother you want her to be. I look forward to our new relationship. Help me to be there for her when she asks but not to interfere when I'm not asked. Help her to lean on you to guide her into her new role.

Help us embrace ________ as a son into our family so he will feel loved and accepted. I ask for your presence and your blessing to be with ________ and ________ on this, their wedding day. Amen.

My Child Is Getting a Divorce

Lord, you see how disappointed I am that my child's marriage has failed. You know the reasons behind it, and you see all the pain our family is suffering because of it. I'm grateful you're in the business of restoring broken hearts and healing damaged families. Help ______ adjust to being single again, and help him/her deal with his/her own feeling of failure.

Give wisdom for how to handle the problems the children will face. Cover all of them with your love and safekeeping. Help me to comfort ______ with love and understanding. Guide me in praying for all of them in the future. I ask this in the name of our Saviour, Amen.

My Daughter Has Been Abused

God, you see the abuse my daughter has suffered, but I'm grateful that you are a God who heals. I ask you to let your healing balm touch her now. Please deal with this man who has inflicted all the wounds.

Help _____ regain her self-worth and see that she is valuable in your eyes. Erase the effects of all the unwholesome and damaging words spoken against her. Give me wisdom to offer her unconditional love in the days ahead, and guide me in praying for her. Protect her from threats and accusations. Lord, she will need you so much. Please give provision, protection, and direction. I ask in Jesus' name, Amen.

For My Grandchildren

Thank you, Lord, for the gift of my grandchildren. I pray for your protection and blessing over each of them … *(call each one by name)*. May they be strong and courageous all through life and not be afraid or terrified. May they know that you, Lord, will go with them and never forsake them (Deuteronomy 31:6). I pray that each grandchild will learn to hear your voice and will follow you all their lives. Amen.

Scriptures to Pray for Children

That Jesus Christ will be formed in our children.

GALATIANS 4:19

That our children—the seed of the righteous—will be delivered from the Evil One.

PROVERBS 11:21 (KJV); MATTHEW 6:13

That our children will be taught of the Lord and their peace will be great. ISAIAH 54:13

That they will train themselves to discern good from evil and have a good conscience toward God. HEBREWS 5:14; 1 PETER 3:21

That God's laws will be in their minds and on their hearts. HEBREWS 8:10

That they will choose companions who are wise, not fools, nor sexually immoral, nor drunkards, nor idolaters, nor slanderers, nor swindlers.

PROVERBS 13:20; 1 CORINTHIANS 5:11

That they will remain sexually pure and keep themselves only for their spouse, asking God for his grace to keep the commitment.

EPHESIANS 5:3, 31-33

That they will honour their parents.

EPHESIANS 6:1-3

Part Four

Praying for My Husband

Thank You for Him

Lord, thank you for my husband. I cherish the years we have had together. Bless his life abundantly. Bless the work of his hands, his labour for us, his family. I thank you for all his good qualities. He's been a good father, a good husband, and a good provider. Show me ways to let him know how much I appreciate him. In Jesus' name, Amen.

Strengthen My Husband in Every Way

Father, bless my husband and our marriage. May he treat me with respect, loving me as Christ loved the church. As a wife, may I be of more worth than rubies to my husband, bringing him good and not harm all the days of our lives. Thank you for this man who is my life partner. Help me to express to him how much I revere and trust him. And, Father, teach me how to pray more effectively for him. I ask in Jesus' name, Amen.

Bless Him in All Areas of Life

My husband needs direction for our family, Lord. Strengthen him to be a wise and loving father to our children. May he increase in favour with you and with his boss and working associates. May he walk in health, having his strength renewed as the eagle's. Thank you for the plans you have for him, Lord. Thank you that you will pour out your blessings on his children and grandchildren. Amen.

Improve Our Communication

Lord, you see the weak links in our marriage that need strengthening. I admit my part in the breakdown in our communication—for my hesitancy to share what's in my heart. Sometimes he seems deaf and uninterested when I try to talk to him. Then I give him the silent treatment. Help me be willing to open up, to be vulnerable, even though I may get hurt. Lord, it seems when I talk, he treats it as idle chitchat. I long to have a strong, happy marriage. To be able to talk freely to this man I married when he was my best friend. Give me practical ways to make our marriage better. To restore the close fellowship we used to enjoy. Thank you, Lord. Amen.

I Forgive Him

Lord, today I choose to forgive my husband for hurting me. Please give me your love with which to love him. He didn't intentionally set out to inflict the wound, but I received it as an arrow aimed at my heart. So now I give you the hurt and ask you to take away the sting. Again, I thank you for this man you gave to me as a marriage partner. Lord, may the Holy Spirit bring your peace to both of us. Amen.

Prayer for a Husband's Job

He needs employment. Lord, open up the right job. May it be one where his skills can best be used. Keep him from discouragement and despair. Help him not to feel inferior and insignificant because he isn't working right now. Show me how to be an encourager to him during this transitional time in his life. Thank you that you will provide for our family's needs—somehow, some way—while he isn't bringing home a salary. I trust you, my Saviour. Amen.

Help Him Be a Good Father

Lord, help my husband be the father you desire him to be. Inspire him to lay aside the newspaper when the children want to talk. Help him to get interested in their hobbies, and care about their studies. Protect him from being a workaholic. Lord, all the hours he spends at his job cannot replace the need we have for him to be physically with us at home—caring about our activities and concerns. Speak to him, Lord, about how brief the time is for us to have the children with us. And how important it is for him to instil in them his own positive attributes. Thank you for hearing me, Lord. Amen.

Gone Away for Awhile

He's gone away this week on a business trip. I miss him so. Put your arms around him, Lord, and keep him safe. Help him with the business contacts he needs. It must be frustrating living out of a suitcase, sleeping in a different hotel room each night. Ease the stress and let him feel your love, acceptance, and favour on his job assignment. Let him know how much I love and admire him. Give him sweet sleep. Awaken him in the morning refreshed, renewed. Thank you, Lord. Amen.

Help Me Not to Complain

Lord, when my husband comes home with dirty clothes and muddy shoes, help me not to complain so much for having to clean up the mess. He works so hard to support our family. Replace my complaining spirit with gratitude and grace. Help the children and me show him our appreciation and encourage him. Thank you, Lord. Amen.

My Husband Doesn't Know You, Lord

Lord, my husband doesn't know you, and it grieves me so. I know you love him, and that Jesus came and died to save the lost. Reveal this truth to him. Open his eyes, Lord, and turn him from darkness to light—so that he may receive forgiveness of sins and an inheritance among those who have been sanctified by faith in you (Acts 26:18). Thank you for working in his life until this prayer is answered. In Jesus' name, Amen.

Help Him See the Light

Heavenly Father, I come to you on behalf of my husband, _______. He seems so vulnerable to being deceived. Guide him in your paths and help him avoid the traps of the Evil One. Give him a desire to read your Word and receive your guidance. Reveal your love to him.

I pray you will send a godly man to share the gospel with him in a way he can understand and receive. Thank you, Lord, for your faithfulness. Amen.

Restore Our Marriage

Father, I bring to you today the broken areas of my marriage and ask you to begin a work of restoration. Forgive me for trying to control my husband instead of committing him to your loving hands. Show me my own wrong attitudes that need to be more loving and Christlike. Lord, I ask you to send across my husband's path a wise counsellor who will speak the Word of God into his life. Reveal your great love to both of us, and extend to us your mercy. Lord, I pray you will restore our marriage and cause our home to bring glory and honour to you. I ask in Jesus' name, Amen.

He Wants a Divorce

Lord, I don't see a way out of this divorce. He wants it. He insists on it. Another woman is waiting in the wings. I am so hurt, and I feel so betrayed, I don't know what to do. Help us both make it through these hard days ahead without more conflict, hurting words, and accusations. Help my husband respond to your truth, Lord. Give me wisdom on how to respond in this crisis, and impart your peace to me. Guide me step by step in the days ahead, and protect me and my children from bitterness. In Jesus' name, Amen.

Scriptures for Meditation

The Lord God said, "It is not good for the man to be alone. I will make a helper suitable for him...." Then the Lord God made a woman from the rib he had taken out of the man, and he brought her to the man. GENESIS 2:18, 20

Husbands, love your wives and do not be harsh with them. COLOSSIANS 3:19

Marriage should be honored by all, and the marriage bed kept pure, for God will judge the adulterer and all the sexually immoral. Keep your lives free from the love of money and be content with what you have, because God has said, "Never will I leave you; never will I forsake you." So we say with confidence, "The Lord is my helper; I will not be afraid. What can man do to me?"

HEBREWS 13:4-6

Husbands, love your wives, just as Christ loved the church and gave himself up for her.... In this same way, husbands ought to love their wives as their own bodies. He who loves his wife loves himself.

EPHESIANS 5:25, 28

Wives, fit in with your husband's plans; for then if they refuse to listen when you talk to them about the Lord, they will be won by your respectful, pure behaviour. Your godly lives will speak to them better than any words.... Be beautiful inside, in your hearts, with the lasting charm of a gentle and quiet spirit which is so precious to God.... You husbands must be careful of your wives, being thoughtful of their needs and honouring them as the weaker sex. Remember that you and your wife are partners in receiving God's blessings, and if you don't treat her as you should, your prayers will not get ready answers.

1 PETER 3:1-2, 4, 7 (TLB)

Part Five

Praying for Family and Friends

Guide Me in Praying for Others

Father, reveal to me by your Holy Spirit and through your Word how to aim my prayers accurately. Thank you for the gift of prayer. Lord, please help me to hit specific targets for your divine will to be accomplished in the lives of relatives and friends for whom I'm praying. I trust you to give me a clear prayer strategy. Strengthen me to be faithful to the task. Thank you in Jesus' name, Amen.

Loved Ones Who Are Lost

Lord, my loved ones ________________ *(name them)* don't know you. The worries of this world, the deceitfulness of riches, and desires for other things have choked the Word of God out of their lives (Mark 4:19). Please create in them a hunger for spiritual truth, and reveal your love to them. Send people across their paths who will share the gospel message with love, power, and conviction.

Lord, your Word says, "The god of this age has blinded the minds of unbelievers, so that they cannot see the light of the gospel ..." (2 Corinthians 4:4). May the blinkers come off! May they see your truth! Lord, I so desperately want them to spend eternity with you. In Jesus' name, Amen.

Stormy Circumstances

Lord, I come to you on behalf of my loved ones who are going through a stormy situation right now. I hang my hope, faith, and trust on your strong right arm reaching out to save. Use me as an instrument of peace and reconciliation in my family. I stand as an intercessor for them, asking you to continue to give me a prayer strategy until they come through this crisis. Just as you quieted the storm for your disciples who were so afraid, I pray you will quiet the storm in the lives of ________. In Jesus' precious name I pray, Amen.

Tough Times for Our Family

How comforting to know you hear us when we cry out to you, Lord. Thank you for your promise to be with our family in our heartbreaking situation. We are trusting you to show yourself strong as our Deliverer and to extend your mercy to all of us. Thank you for your grace that has brought us this far and for the love that binds our family together. We offer you the sacrifice of praise in the midst of our tough times, knowing you will receive all glory in the end. Amen.

Away from Home

I'm away from my family for a few days. Already I'm missing them. But, Lord, help me not to miss what you have in mind for me on this trip. I believe you're ordering my steps, and I want to embrace each moment, each experience. Help me to be sensitive to your leading, Lord, and strengthen me to fulfil your purpose. Thank you that you will protect me on this journey and return me home safely. In Jesus' name, Amen.

Prayer for My Colleagues

Lord, I come to you on behalf of the people I work with day by day. You see their needs and the problems they struggle with. Please reveal your love to them. Help them to understand that following in your ways will solve many of their difficulties.

Father, help me to be a friend to those who are open to receive your love. Help me to reflect your character in my relationships on the job—whether with my boss, my peers, or those I supervise. I'm willing to be your ambassador in my workplace, Lord, as you provide your grace and wisdom. Thank you for your guidance. Amen.

May I Love My Parents Well

Thank you, Lord, for the parents you have given me. Help me to honour them in the way you intended for parents to be honoured by their children. I admit there are times when I've been disappointed in them and by them. And I've failed them, too. Let your love flow through us, one to another. Help us to forgive one another just as Christ in God forgives us. Give them strength, wisdom, and improved health. I ask in Jesus' name, Amen.

I Forgive My Parents

Lord, I forgive my parents for all the things they did and the words they spoke that wounded my spirit. Some of these hurts are so deeply buried that I haven't admitted them to anyone. I ask you to heal these wounds. Not only do I choose to forgive them, Lord, but I ask you to forgive them, too. I pray your perfect will be done in their lives. Father, restore our broken relationship. Forgive me for the things I've said or thought against them that were dishonouring to them or displeasing to you. I am truly sorry.

Now, Lord, I receive your forgiveness. Thank you, heavenly Father, for the cleansing that it brings. Thank you that when I forgive, you forgive me, too. In Jesus' name, Amen.

My Parents Are Aging

Lord, help my parents fight the good fight of faith and finish the course you've appointed for them. It hurts me so much to see them grow feeble and suffer with infirmities. I commit them into your loving care. Only you know the number of their days. I thank you that because they know Jesus, they will one day be with him—in a place where their minds and bodies won't be affected by disease.

As much as I love them, I realize they are nearing the end of their lives. Help me release them when their time for entering heaven comes. Give me the patience, kindness, and gentleness I need to respond in love to their needs. Thank you, loving Father. Amen.

My Parents Don't Know You, Lord

Lord, I'm grieved because my parents haven't accepted Jesus as their Saviour. I know it is not your will that anyone perish. I stand in the gap in prayer for them. God, have mercy on them, and send your Holy Spirit to bring them to Jesus. Please grant them repentance leading to the knowledge of truth (2 Peter 3:9; 2 Timothy 2:25). Thank you for revealing your love and mercy to them. In Jesus' name, Amen.

For Sins That Harass Our Family

Lord Jesus, thank you for redeeming us "from the curse of the law by becoming a curse for us" (Galatians 3:13). I boldly ask that in your mercy you would forgive the sins which have caused such great pain in our family. Lord, some of these sin patterns have harassed our family for generations. Bring your healing to those who are suffering. Thank you for the blessings and gifts that have come from my ancestry, but I trust you now to weaken those negative traits that aren't pleasing to you and uproot them. Thank you for your love and faithfulness. Amen.

Bless Our Family and Home

Father, we ask your blessing upon our family and our home. Put your shield of protection around all who live and visit here, guarding us from evil and from harm. May your holy presence abide here.

I speak Aaron's priestly blessing over my family: "The Lord bless you and keep you; the Lord make his face shine upon you and be gracious to you; the Lord turn his face towards you and give you peace" (Numbers 6:24). Amen.

Healing of a Loved One

Father, my loved one ______*(name)* is ill. I come boldly to your throne of grace, asking that he/she receive mercy and grace in time of need (Hebrews 4:16). Lord, I ask you to heal his/her body, causing it to function properly. Give complete restoration to his/her soul and spirit, and grant wisdom to those who are caring for him/her. I pray there will be no complications during his/her recovery, and no adverse reaction to medications. May Jesus the Great Physician heal ______*(name)* just as he healed the sick when he was on earth. I thank you, Lord. Amen.

Scriptures for Meditation

"Don't be afraid of them. Remember the Lord, who is great and awesome, and fight for your brothers, your sons and your daughters, your wives and your homes." NEHEMIAH 4:14b

Surely he took up our infirmities and carried our sorrows, yet we considered him stricken by God, smitten by him, and afflicted. But he was pierced for our transgressions, he was crushed for our iniquities; the punishment that brought us peace was upon him, and by his wounds we are healed.

ISAIAH 53:4-5

He himself bore our sins in his body on the tree, so that we might die to sins and live for righteousness; by his wounds you have been healed. For you were like sheep going astray, but now you have returned to the Shepherd and Overseer of your souls. 1 PETER 2:24-25

This is what the Lord says: "Restrain your voice from weeping and your eyes from tears, for your work will be rewarded," declares the Lord. "They will return from the land of the enemy. So there is hope for your future," declares the Lord. "Your children will return to their own land."

JEREMIAH 31:16-17

The Lord is not slow in keeping his promise, as some understand slowness. He is patient with you, not wanting anyone to perish, but everyone to come to repentance. 2 PETER 3:9

If you confess with your mouth, "Jesus is Lord," and believe in your heart that God raised him from the dead, you will be saved. For it is with your heart that you believe and are justified, and it is with your mouth that you confess and are saved. ROMANS 10:9-10

If we confess our sins, he is faithful and just and will forgive us our sins and purify us from all unrighteousness. 1 JOHN 1:9

Part Six

Prayers Singles Pray

Lord, I Need a Friend

Lord, you know how lonely I am some days. Whether I ever get married or not, I need companionship, friendship. Thank you for my job and the financial blessings it provides. Thank you for my outside interests that stimulate me. But, Lord, I need new relationships—people who will care about me for who I am, not for what I can do for them. But I want friends who like being with me just because I'm me. Lord, fill this lonely place in my heart. I ask in Jesus' name, Amen.

It's Not Easy Being Single

Lord, those who say it's easy to be single don't know all I face. I have secret desires. I fight sexual feelings. I try to stay in good company to avoid temptation. But, Lord, you know my heart. You know my thoughts. Please help me be the woman of God you want me to be, fulfilling your purpose for my life. Help me embrace this season of life with enthusiasm, not regret or remorse. May I be an encourager to those you put in my path. I long to be a blessing to others, Lord. Amen.

Thank You for My Family

Lord, I thank you for my life right now. Although I live alone, I'm not lonely. I have a wonderful extended family. Thank you for my brothers and sisters. Though they are all married, they have made a place for me in their families. Thank you for the opportunity to shower my love on my nieces and nephews—enjoying their birthday celebrations and special occasions. I am truly blessed. I praise you, Lord. Amen.

Single Again

Single again. I never thought this would happen. Lord, help me adjust to this new state of singleness, and all that this change in my life will entail. I can hardly remember what it was like to be single. Right now my biggest concern is financial—managing wisely what I have to live on. I have so many decisions all at once—disposing of property in the right way, deciding where to live, finding a job.... Oh, God, help me to make wise choices, not foolish ones I'll later regret. I'm depending on you to see me through, Lord. Amen.

A New Relationship

There's a special man in my life right now, Lord. I need your help to keep our relationship what you want it to be—no more and no less. I don't know whether what I feel for him is real love or just infatuation springing out of my deep longing for a meaningful relationship. And I'm not sure what his intentions are towards me. Lord, keep me from reading into his actions a deeper interest than he really feels. Don't let me miss your best, Father. I don't want to pursue a relationship that doesn't have your blessing. Protect my heart, and reveal your will to me. I ask in Jesus' name, Amen.

Help Me Reach Out to Others

Lord, forgive me for being so focused on my own problems that I sometimes fail to reach out to others. I choose today to release my own needs into your loving hands. Help me to continue making this choice each day—I know your ways are perfect, and you are able to do exceedingly beyond what I could ask or think. I want to be a channel of blessing to others as the Holy Spirit pours your love through me. Lord, I'm willing to be your hands extended to those in need. Please show me the ones you want me to touch. In Jesus' name, Amen.

Scriptures for Meditation

Find rest, O my soul, in God alone; my hope comes from him. He alone is my rock and my salvation; he is my fortress, I will not be shaken. My salvation and my honour depend on God; he is my mighty rock, my refuge. PSALM 62:5-7

Sing to God, sing praise to his name, extol him who rides on the clouds—his name is the Lord—and rejoice before him. A father to the fatherless, a defender of widows, is God in his holy dwelling. God sets the lonely in families, he leads forth the prisoners with singing. PSALM 68:4-6

If you spend yourselves in behalf of the hungry and satisfy the needs of the oppressed, then your light will rise in the darkness, and your night will become like the noonday. ISAIAH 58:10

"My soul glorifies the Lord and my spirit rejoices in God my Saviour, for he has been mindful of the humble state of his servant. From now on all generations will call me blessed, for the Mighty One has done great things for me—holy is his name. His mercy extends to those who fear him, from generation to generation." LUKE 1:46-50

An unmarried woman or virgin is concerned about the Lord's affairs: Her aim is to be devoted to the Lord in both body and spirit. But a married woman is concerned about the affairs of this world—how she can please her husband.

1 CORINTHIANS 7:34

God has given each of you some special abilities; be sure to use them to help each other, passing on to others God's many kinds of blessings.

1 PETER 4:10 (TLB)

Part Seven

Praying through Tough Times

Balancing Home and Work

Lord, I'm doing my best to balance home and work. Sometimes I feel there's not enough of me to go around in meeting all the demands. Both my energy and the clock run out before I can get it all done. And when I get really frazzled, the people I love most bear the brunt of my frustration. Help me, Lord, to draw from your strength and peace in ordering my priorities. Help me to use my tongue wisely and always with kindness (Proverbs 31:26). Equip me to be the best I can be, both at home and on the job, and bring people into my life who can help me with what I need to do. Thank you for your provision, Lord. Amen.

Help Me Get through the Day

Lord, show me the way out of this dark time. I am so depressed. Please keep me from falling apart. I feel hopeless, dead inside. Unable to see myself getting through another day. Lord, heal my heart and help me cling to hope. All the words of encouragement I've heard seem so stale. I throw myself on your mercy. Jesus, rescue me! Amen.

Sleep Escapes Me

I am tormented with sleeplessness, Lord. Tossing and turning hour after hour. Fretful and worried. I lie awake imagining "What if this happens?" or "What if that happens?" Help me turn over to you all my "What if's." I choose to fix my mind on you, to trust in you, and embrace your promise that "you will keep me in perfect peace" (Isaiah 26:3). Come, calm my anxious thoughts. Thank you that because you "neither slumber nor sleep" (Psalm 121:3-4), I can now fall asleep with your comforting presence. Thank you that your angels are watching over me. I love you, Lord. Amen.

I Don't Understand, Lord

I don't at all understand the tough times I'm going through right now, Lord. But I release to you my own desires and expectations in this situation. I declare your lordship over my life, and I choose to believe that you love me. Show me the attitudes I need to change, and enable me to do it. Thank you that in the unseen realm, you are working in people and events in a way that ultimately will bring you glory. Lord, my faith is in you, not in my circumstances. Help me see these things from your viewpoint and then walk in your peace. Amen.

My Cloud of Depression Is Lifting

Lord, thank you that I don't have to live under a cloud of depression. I praise you that you are at work even now, restoring the joy of my salvation. And healing my soul—my mind, will, and emotions. Help me keep my eyes on my Redeemer and not upon my problems. May I find my comfort and my healing in you, Lord. Amen.

Nothing Is Impossible

Lord, help me see as you see, speak as you speak, and act as you act. Remind me that to declare something hopeless is to say I have a helpless God. May I learn to trust you even when my situation appears to be beyond remedy. Nothing is impossible with you. You are bigger than any mountain I may face. Thank you, Lord, for those who are praying for me. And thank you for giving me the strength to stand through this trial. I'm trusting you for victory! Amen.

Walk Me through My Pain

Thank you, Lord, for your precious Holy Spirit, who is my Comforter. Walk me through my pain, disappointment, betrayal, sorrow, and suffering. Surround me with your presence, and hide me in the shelter of your wings. Help me to trust that you have the bigger picture of my life's circumstances and to lay aside my own expectations when they are not from your heart. I choose to cast my cares, worries, and disappointments on you, knowing you care for me. Thank you for your comfort. Amen.

Falsely Accused

Lord, you said no weapon formed against us shall prosper—that is our inheritance. Thank you that no tongue that speaks against us will do permanent harm (Isaiah 54:17). I ask that in our crisis—in which we have been falsely accused and grossly misunderstood—righteousness will prevail.

May the Holy Spirit, our Advocate, give us wisdom as to what to say and when to say it. We pray for ourselves and those representing us in court that we would have wisdom in knowing how to respond. May you be glorified in this. Lord, we look to you to protect our finances and help us to be good stewards of your provision. Thank you for proving your faithfulness to us. Amen.

You Are My Rock

Father, I acknowledge to you my pain, my anger, my sadness, and my sense of feeling overwhelmed. I take refuge in you, Lord, because you're the Rock I can run to. I'm putting myself in your hands. Guide me through this process of grief and sorrow, and allow me to move at my own pace.

Father, I trust you for total restoration of body, soul, and spirit. Thank you for being my confidence, firm and strong, and for keeping me from being caught in the enemy's hidden pitfalls. I choose to trust you, even though I don't understand. Thank you for the comfort of your Holy Spirit. In Jesus' name, Amen.

I'm So Disappointed, Lord

Father, this disappointment is almost more than I can bear. You promised that the Holy Spirit would comfort us. You said others would comfort us. I need the assurance of that comfort. Thank you that you know the road ahead of me and will order my steps. Help me to trust you in these uncertain times and to walk in the confidence of your love for me.

I refuse to allow the enemy to steal my joy. Lord, my joy is in you and does not depend upon favourable circumstances. Thank you that you alone are my source of life, for you alone bore the pain of every hurt I will ever have to endure. I rejoice in you today. Amen.

I Lost a Child

Lord, I never thought I'd outlive my child. What anguish and heartache I feel. What emptiness. How will I make it without this beautiful one who filled my life so full of joy?

Thank you that you have prepared a place for ________ in heaven. How I praise you for the treasure he/she was to me. God, I know you understand all that we go through in these painful times. But my grief is so deep, I can't even express the extent of my loss. Lord, comfort me. I know you will never leave me nor forsake me. Please make that real to me, even now. Especially now! Amen.

Exchanging Self-Pity for Hope

God, thank you that you make no mistakes, and for the assurance you are with us now—whether we're in joy or in sadness. Lord, you promised to give joy in the morning, and you demonstrated it on Resurrection Day. You suffered our sorrows. You understand. And through you, Lord, we have eternal life and hope. Guard us from self-pity, but help us to walk in that hope today—keeping our eyes fixed upon you. Thank you, Lord. Amen.

My Friend Has Died

My friend died last week, and I admit I am at a loss for words. Thank you for the years we had together—the laughs and tears we shared, the visits and the trips we made together, the early morning prayer times that were so special. What a rich deposit she made into my life. I still can hear her laugh, see her smile, and even remember times when we disagreed.

Bring comfort to her bereaved family as they deal with their feelings of emptiness and loneliness. Reassure them of your love. May the memories we have of her be a rainbow of hope as we walk through the sorrow of the moment. Thank you, Lord, that we will be together again in your presence. Amen.

My Husband Is Gone

Lord, I'm struggling with my anger because this loss seems so unfair. Sometimes I hold on to self-pity—then I'm overwhelmed with guilt about my feelings. Please settle my emotions in the midst of this confusion, Lord, and give me your peace and comfort. You said you would never leave me nor forsake me; I cling to that promise today.

Now that he's gone, I depend totally on you, Lord, to be my husband and the father to my children. I know somehow you will provide for my needs. I trust you, heavenly Father, and commit these, my most pressing needs, to you:

financial: ______________________________
physical: ________________________________
spiritual: ______________________________
emotional: _____________________________

Help me keep my focus on you while walking through this valley. I ask in Jesus' name, Amen.

Scriptures for Meditation

The righteous cry and the Lord hears, and delivers them out of all their troubles. The Lord is near to the brokenhearted and saves those who are crushed in spirit. Many are the afflictions of the righteous; but the Lord delivers him out of them all.

PSALM 34:17-19 (NASB)

Trust in the Lord with all your heart and lean not on your own understanding; in all your ways acknowledge him, and he will make your paths straight.

PROVERBS 3:5-6

But let all those who take refuge and put their trust in You rejoice; let them ever sing and shout for joy, because You make a covering over them and defend them; let those also who love Your name be joyful in You and be in high spirits.

PSALM 5:11 (AMPLIFIED)

I love the Lord, for he heard my voice; he heard my cry for mercy. Because he turned his ear to me, I will call on him as long as I live.... The

Lord is gracious and righteous; our God is full of compassion. The Lord protects the simple-hearted; when I was in great need, he saved me. Be at rest once more, O my soul, for the Lord has been good to you. For you, O Lord, have delivered my soul from death, my eyes from tears, my feet from stumbling, that I may walk before the Lord in the land of the living. PSALM 116:1-2, 5-9

I lift up my eyes to the hills—where does my help come from? My help comes from the Lord, the Maker of heaven and earth. He will not let your foot slip—he who watches over you will not slumber; indeed, he who watches over Israel will neither slumber nor sleep. The Lord watches over you—the Lord is your shade at your right hand; the sun will not harm you by day, nor the moon by night. The Lord will keep you from all harm—he will watch over your life; the Lord will watch over your coming and going both now and forevermore. PSALM 121

Those who sow in tears will reap with songs of joy. He who goes out weeping, carrying seed to sow, will return with songs of joy, carrying sheaves with him. PSALM 126:5-6

The Lord upholds all those who fall and lifts up all who are bowed down.... The Lord is near to all who call on him, to all who call on him in truth.
PSALM 145:14, 18

For the Lamb at the centre of the throne will be their shepherd; he will lead them to springs of living water. And God will wipe away every tear from their eyes.
REVELATION 7:17

Part Eight

When I Am Afraid

Lord, I Need a Job

I'm trying not to be anxious about this, Lord, but I'm coming to you with my need for a job. You understand all that has brought me to this crossroad. It's a scary place to be. Forgive my failures, Lord, and help me avoid those mistakes in the future.

I know you've not given me a spirit of fear. Your Word says you have given me a spirit of "power and of love and of a sound mind" (2 Timothy 1:7, NKJV). Help me to move ahead with confidence in you, trusting you to guide me and give me favour to find the right job. Thank you, Lord. Amen.

I Cast My Worry on You

Father, thank you for the promises for provision in your Word. I acknowledge you as the source of everything I need for my spirit, soul, and body. Lord, help me to set aside worry and instead trust you for all my needs. I thank you for the degree of health you've given me and for the resources you provide. Help me to be a good steward of all your gifts. Lord, show me ways I can be generous in reaching out to others with needs greater than mine. I praise you for your faithfulness. Amen.

You Are My Refuge

Lord, may I always dwell in your shelter, for you are my refuge and my fortress. You are my God. You will answer me when I am in trouble and deliver me. My hope and trust are in you, Lord. You are my stronghold and my deliverer—the strong tower I run to for safety. Whenever I am afraid you are there watching over me. My life, my reputation, is in your hands. Thank you for the favour and care you bestow on your children. I praise you for your mighty works! Amen.

Victory over Fear

Heavenly Father, help me to lean on your strong arm when I am afraid. Give me a greater confidence in you, my Good Shepherd, so I can say I fear no evil. I desire to become totally secure in your love—the kind of love that never lets go. Help me to set aside worry and replace it with trust. And to remember that Christ's resurrection destroys the enemy's power to make me afraid. Help me every day to walk in this new level of faith. I ask in Jesus' name, Amen.

Scriptures for Meditation

You are my hiding place; you will protect me from trouble and surround me with songs of deliverance. PSALM 32:7

When I am afraid, I will trust in you. In God, whose word I praise, in God I trust; I will not be afraid. What can mortal man do to me?

PSALM 56:3-4

You guide me with your counsel, and afterwards you will take me into glory. Whom have I in heaven but you? And earth has nothing I desire besides you. My flesh and my heart may fail, but God is the strength of my heart and my portion for ever. PSALM 73:24-26

But blessed is the man who trusts in the Lord, whose confidence is in him. He will be like a tree planted by the water that sends out its roots by the stream. It does not fear when heat comes; its leaves are always green. It has no worries in a year of drought and never fails to bear fruit.

JEREMIAH 17:7-8

So do not fear, for I am with you; do not be dismayed, for I am your God. I will strengthen you and help you; I will uphold you with my righteous right hand. ISAIAH 41:10

"Therefore I tell you, do not worry about your life, what you will eat or drink; or about your body, what you will wear. Is not life more important than food, and the body more important than clothes?... But seek first his kingdom and his righteousness, and all these things will be given to you as well. Therefore do not worry about tomorrow, for tomorrow will worry about itself. Each day has enough trouble of its own."

MATTHEW 6:25, 33-34

Do not be anxious about anything, but in everything, by prayer and petition, with thanksgiving, present your requests to God. And the peace of God, which transcends all understanding, will guard your hearts and your minds in Christ Jesus.

PHILIPPIANS 4:6-7

There is no fear in love. But perfect love drives out fear, because fear has to do with punishment. The one who fears is not made perfect in love.

1 JOHN 4:18

Part Nine

Prayers of Thanksgiving and Praise

Worthy of Worship

Today, Lord, I realize how little time I spend in worshipping you. One sentence in a book stabbed my heart:

*We work too long, play too fast, laugh too loud, and worship too little.**

I worship you, Lord, for you are worthy of all praise. I worship you—not because of what you do for me but because of who you are. Creator God. Redeemer. Saviour. Lord. Deliverer. Protector. The Almighty. Alpha and Omega—the beginning and the end. When I worship you, my problems seem so small compared to your greatness. I give you praise, Mighty God! Amen.

*Richard Exley, *The Rhythm of Life* (Tulsa, Okla.: Honor Books, 1987), 108.

Joining Heaven's Choir

Lord, I join the creatures around the throne of God as they never stop saying:

"Holy, holy, holy
is the Lord God Almighty,
who was, and is, and is to come."

REVELATION 4:8

And I add my song to angels encircling your throne as they sing with loud voices:

"Worthy is the Lamb, who was slain,
to receive power and wealth and wisdom and strength and honour and glory and praise!"

REVELATION 5:12b

A Brand-New Year

I thank you for the year that's passed, Lord. For my family and my home, for protection. Most of all, I thank you that I've grown so much closer to you. Last year's trials were fierce. I couldn't have made it through without your strength and direction.

How thankful I am as I look at a brand-new calendar's blank pages to be filled in. I greet the new year with immense anticipation and expectation. Let's make it the best ever, Lord. Don't let me miss your divine appointments or your plan for my life in the months ahead. I praise you in Jesus' name, Amen.

Thank You for Spring

Something wonderful is happening inside me, Lord. Today the grass looks greener, the sky more blue—and I saw my first daffodils. Just because I stopped to take a closer look. In all my hurrying about to do my chores, I often neglect to take time to appreciate the natural beauty around me.

Your creation is so gorgeous, Father! Forgive me for taking spring for granted. It reminds me that through the winter, you've been working beneath the surface of the cold, hard ground. And now we see trees budding, flowers blooming, and hear birds singing. Thank you for the beautiful earth. Thank you for your faithfulness. Amen.

I Will Praise You, Regardless

Lord, I praise you for the hard times, as well as for the good. During my fiery trials I'm being refined like gold. It's painful, and I struggle to endure the process. But I choose to praise you—because you, as a loving Father, know how to remove the impurities and bring out the best in me. I praise you for loving me so much that you don't give up on me. Regardless of my discomfort and impatience, I trust you, Lord. And I praise and worship you with all my heart. Amen.

Thank You That Mourning Is Over

Tonight I was floundering in sorrow and mourning, Lord. But you came with your presence to comfort and reassure me of your love. How I thank you! I make this psalm my own proclamation:

You turned my wailing into dancing;
you removed my sackcloth and clothed me with joy,
that my heart may sing to you and not be silent.
O Lord my God, I will give you thanks for ever.

PSALM 30:11-12

Praise you, Lord. Amen.

Thanksgiving Prayer

Lord, if I were to count my blessings and name them one by one, it would take a very long time! My heart overflows with gratitude. I offer thanks especially for ______________ *(name the special blessings that come to mind)*. Even in times of difficulty, we have seen your hand at work. Your grace is always sufficient for the need. Lord, the hard times make us even more grateful for your intervention. May we not forget to reach out to those in need. We offer you our praise. Amen.

Scriptures for Praise and Worship

"Praise be to you, O Lord, God of our father Israel, from everlasting to everlasting. Yours, O Lord, is the greatness and the power and the glory and the majesty and the splendour, for everything in heaven and earth is yours. Yours, O Lord, is the kingdom; you are exalted as head over all." 1 CHRONICLES 29:10-11

The heavens declare the glory of God; the skies proclaim the work of his hands. Day after day they pour forth speech; night after night they display knowledge. PSALM 19:1-2

I will praise you for ever for what you have done; in your name I will hope, for your name is good. I will praise you in the presence of your saints.

PSALM 52:9

Praise be to his glorious name for ever; may the whole earth be filled with his glory. Amen and Amen. PSALM 72:19

I will praise you, O Lord my God, with all my heart; I will glorify your name for ever.

PSALM 86:12

I will exalt you, my God the King; I will praise your name for ever and ever. Every day I will praise you and extol your name for ever and ever. Great is the Lord and most worthy of praise; his greatness no one can fathom. PSALM 145:1-3

Praise the Lord. Sing to the Lord a new song, his praise in the assembly of the saints.... For the Lord takes delight in his people; he crowns the humble with salvation. Let the saints rejoice in this honour and sing for joy on their beds. May the praise of God be in their mouths and a double-edged sword in their hands. PSALM 149:1, 4-6

Praise the Lord. Praise God in his sanctuary; praise him in his mighty heavens. Praise him for his acts of power; praise him for his surpassing greatness. Praise him with the sounding of the trumpet, praise him with the harp and lyre, praise him with tambourine and dancing, praise him with the strings and flute, praise him with the clash of cymbals, praise him with resounding cymbals. Let everything that has breath praise the Lord. Praise the Lord. PSALM 150

Rejoice in the Lord always. I will say it again: Rejoice! PHILIPPIANS 4:4

Through Jesus, therefore, let us continually offer to God a sacrifice of praise—the fruit of lips that confess his name. HEBREWS 13:15

"You are worthy, our Lord and God, to receive glory and honour and power, for you created all things, and by your will they were created and have their being." REVELATION 4:11

Part Ten

Purify My Life

I Complained Today

Lord, forgive me for grumbling and complaining. I'm not unlike the Israelites, dissatisfied with what you provided for them so generously in the wilderness. I'm sorry I haven't had a grateful heart. My situation could be much worse. Forgive me. Thank you for all your hand has provided for me over and over again. You are worthy of praise, Lord! Amen.

Not My Will but Yours

Lord, I repent for insisting upon my own way and trying to run my own life, or someone else's. Forgive me for thinking I know better than you. Help me learn to take "hands off"—trusting you with the plan and purpose you have for me and for my loved ones. I don't want to have selfish ambition for myself, my child, my spouse, my parents, or anyone close to me.

Lord, forgive me for trying to control other people with my desires or with the words I've spoken. Please remind me when I fall back into the old pattern. Lord, I truly desire to change and to choose your way. Amen.

Shine Your Light into My Dark Corners

Lord, show me the dark corners of my heart that I need to open up to your light. Give me the courage to allow your grace to heal and restore those areas I've tried to keep hidden. Help me to co-operate with the Holy Spirit; strengthen me to stand against the enemy. I acknowledge that I can't do this by myself. I renounce my pride and ask for your help. Thank you for setting me free. In Jesus' name, Amen.

Make Me Like You

Lord, help me each day to choose to reflect your character. I want to be continually transformed into your likeness. Let me be more concerned about pleasing you than wanting to change my circumstances or the people around me. Help me to find my identity in you rather than in what I do or where I live. Holy Spirit, I give you permission to change me from the inside out. Thank you that you will do it with your tender love and in your timing. Amen.

Clothe Me in Your Strength

Lord, I truly desire to be a woman of strength and dignity. Empowered by your Spirit, joyful in the unique image you've created me to be. Help me to exchange my weakness for your strength. Thank you that your strength will enable me to become a dynamic woman walking in your love and blessing. Lord, I want your great love to flow through me to others. Help me to keep the channel clear. I ask in Jesus' name, Amen.

Wipe My Slate Clean

Thank you, Jesus, for coming to earth to die as a sin offering for me. Whenever I sin and am burdened by the guilt of it, I need only come to you with true repentance and you wipe my sin-slate clean. Thank you for cleansing me by your precious blood, restoring me to fellowship with the Father.

What an exchange. What a release. What a gift! Praise you, Lord. May I continue to walk in your freedom and to help set other captives free. Thank you. Amen.

Guilty No More

Lord, I confess to you how badly I did today—the sharp words, ugly attitude, my resentment for what I had to endure. It was not pleasing to you or to me. Forgive me, Lord. Thank you for not condemning me. Thank you for helping me to make a fresh start in your strength. How grateful I am that your grace frees me from guilt and condemnation. I rejoice in you! Amen.

When I Have Failed You, Lord

The testing of my faith works endurance. Lord, I'm not good at testings or endurance. How many times I've disappointed you, disappointed myself, and been a poor student at enduring. I didn't like it when my (friend, boss, neighbour...) spoke back so harshly. My attitude was rotten, my reaction not Christlike. I failed the test. But tomorrow is another day. And you always give hope for tomorrow, Lord! I'll do my best to pass. Amen.

Overcoming Sin

God, forgive me for the selfish sins I have willingly embraced. I confess I have lived for my own pleasure and have rebelled against your ways. Please cleanse me and make me whole, and help me abstain from evil. My prayer is that you will purify me—separate me from worldly pursuits—and fill me with your Holy Spirit. Lord, may my spirit, soul, and body be preserved complete and blameless at the day of your coming (1 Thessalonians 5:22-23). Thank you for setting me free! Amen.

Resisting Temptation

Lord, your Word assures me that no temptation I face is irresistible. Thank you for your promise that you are faithful to give me strength to overcome the enemy's enticement (1 Corinthians 10:13). Father, I confess that when I have yielded to temptation, it was because I failed to keep my heart fixed upon you. Forgive me, Lord, for going my own selfish way. Help me to turn away from the world's fascination and to walk in your love. Amen.

Protect Me from the Evil One

Father, just as Jesus prayed that you would protect his disciples from the Evil One, I ask that you also protect me by the power of Jesus' name. Reveal to me any area of my life where I've not obeyed you. Thank you for the forgiveness and protection you provide through the blood Jesus shed on the cross. I rejoice in your victory! Amen.

Thank You for the Holy Spirit

Lord, thank you for your incredible gift of the Holy Spirit. Forgive me for not giving attention, as I should, to this gift you've provided. I want to experience your presence. To sense your unconditional love. To know you more intimately. Thank you that you will reveal yourself to me in this way through the Holy Spirit. I give you praise for all your gifts! Amen.

Direct My Path

Lord, forgive me for the times I've failed to wait for your direction and walked in my own strength. Thank you for your faithfulness in redeeming my mistakes. Lord, help me tune out the clamour of the world, the flesh, and the devil and discipline myself to listen for your still, small voice.

Speak by your Holy Spirit, leading me to the divine appointments of your choosing. I want to stay on the path that follows your footsteps, Lord. Help me avoid the pitfalls of spiritual pride, selfishness, unforgiveness, or speaking unkind words. I pray that my walk and my words will honour and glorify you. In Jesus' name, Amen.

My Spiritual Gifts

Lord, your Word tells us that David didn't die until he had served your purpose for his generation (Acts 13:36). I pray you will enable me to identify and acknowledge the spiritual gifts you've given me, equipping me to fulfil your purposes. Remove from me any hindrances preventing your purposes from being fulfilled. Thank you, Father, for these gracious gifts which allow me to minister to others. Amen.

Let Me Bear Fruit

You may pray this prayer, based on Colossians 1:9-12 and Romans 15:13, for yourself. You may also pray it for someone else by inserting the appropriate name and changing the pronouns.

Lord, I ask you to fill me with the knowledge of your will and all spiritual wisdom and understanding. Help me live a life worthy of you, Lord, pleasing you in every way. Help me bear fruit in every good work, growing in the knowledge of God. Strengthen me with all power according to your glorious might so that I may have great endurance and patience, joyfully giving thanks to you, Father, for you have qualified me to share in the inheritance of the saints in the kingdom of light. Lord, I pray that you, the God of hope, will fill me with all joy and peace as I trust in you, so that I may overflow with hope by the power of the Holy Spirit. Amen.

Scriptures for the Overcomer

You will keep in perfect peace him whose mind is steadfast, because he trusts in you. Trust in the Lord for ever, for the Lord, the Lord, is the Rock eternal.

ISAIAH 26:3-4

Create in me a pure heart, O God, and renew a steadfast spirit within me. Do not cast me from your presence or take your Holy Spirit from me. Restore to me the joy of your salvation and grant me a willing spirit, to sustain me.

PSALM 51:10-12

We should not be like cringing, fearful slaves, but we should behave like God's very own children, adopted into the bosom of his family, and calling to him, "Father, Father." For his Holy Spirit speaks to us deep in our hearts, and tells us that we really are God's children. And since we are his children, we will share his treasures—for all God gives to his Son Jesus is now ours too. But if we are to share his glory, we must also share his suffering.

ROMANS 8:15-17 (TLB)

Do not conform any longer to the pattern of this world, but be transformed by the renewing of your mind. Then you will be able to test and approve what God's will is—his good, pleasing and perfect will. ROMANS 12:2

Submit yourselves, then, to God. Resist the devil, and he will flee from you. Come near to God and he will come near to you. Wash your hands, you sinners, and purify your hearts, you double-minded.... Humble yourselves before the Lord, and he will lift you up. JAMES 4:7-8,10

The Lord is the Spirit who gives them life, and where he is there is freedom.... But we Christians have no veil over our faces; we can be mirrors that brightly reflect the glory of the Lord. And as the Spirit of the Lord works within us, we become more and more like him.

2 CORINTHIANS 3:17-18 (TLB)

Since we have these promises, dear friends, let us purify ourselves from everything that contaminates body and spirit, perfecting holiness out of reverence for God. 2 CORINTHIANS 7:1

I pray that out of his glorious riches he may strengthen you with power through his Spirit in your inner being, so that Christ may dwell in your hearts through faith. EPHESIANS 3:16-17a

Part Eleven

When I Need to Forgive

I Am Angry, Lord

Heavenly Father, I admit to you that I am angry with ________ because ________ *(name the offence)*. I feel what he/she did is wrong, and I feel violated. Thank you that I can freely express this to you now. But, Lord, by an act of my will, I choose to forgive this person. Forgive me, Lord, for the thoughts of bitterness and revenge I've allowed to take hold of my heart and for the angry words I've spoken. I release this anger and choose to identify with you and your ways. Thank you for your cleansing.

I pray as King David did, "Set a guard over my mouth, O Lord; keep watch over the door of my lips" (Psalm 141:3). Help me to obey you, to walk in love, and to co-operate with the Holy Spirit in controlling my tongue and resolving this conflict. In Jesus' name, Amen.

Help Me Forgive Those Who Hurt Me

Lord Jesus, you knew rejection, abandonment, pain, and betrayal by those close to you, so you can identify with my hurts and wounds. Yet, Lord, as you hung on that cross, bleeding and dying from wounds you didn't deserve, you actually asked your Father to forgive your offenders. Lord, please help me forgive each person who has rejected, wounded, or abused me. I honestly don't feel some of them deserve forgiveness. But I want my relationship with you to be right, so I choose to forgive ________ *(name)* and set myself free. I ask you to judge him/her according to your mercy, and to grant him/her healing and release from bondage.

Lord, please heal my painful memories. Help me anticipate with joy what you have in store for my life. Thank you for your promise that you will complete the work of healing you've begun in me (Philippians 1:6). Give me strength to continue to walk in your love and forgiveness. I ask in Jesus' name, Amen.

Help Me Show Mercy

Lord, I truly mean it when I pray, "Forgive us our debts, as we also have forgiven our debtors" (Matthew 6:12). Thank you for helping me work my way through the process of forgiving those who have wounded me. Thank you for the mercy you have shown by forgiving all my sins. Please, Lord, help me show mercy to others. Help me choose to forgive each time a painful memory comes back or whenever someone offends me. I rejoice in the freedom forgiveness brings to my life! Amen.

I Am Forgiven

Lord, forgive me for not truly believing the blood of Jesus was sufficient to cover my sins. I know you have forgiven me; I accept that forgiveness and I choose to forgive myself, too. I refuse to listen to the lies of the accuser any longer. Heavenly Father, I stand on your Word and declare that because I have confessed my sins to you, you have forgiven and cleansed me. Thank you for such reassurance. I praise you for allowing Jesus to die for me. What an all-sufficient, forgiving Father you are to me! I love you and worship you. Amen.

I Want to Mend This Broken Relationship

Lord, give me the wisdom to help repair breaches and mend broken relationships. I don't want to be a party to dissension and strife. Help me break down walls of enmity and be a peace-maker. I want to be pleasing to you and a good example to others. Keep my mouth from deceit and malice. Help me, with the strength only you can provide, to walk in your compassion. Amen.

Scriptures for Meditation

What a difference between man's sin and God's forgiveness! For this one man, Adam, brought death to many through his sin. But this one man, Jesus Christ, brought forgiveness to many through God's mercy. Adam's one sin brought the penalty of death to many, while Christ freely takes away many sins and gives glorious life instead. ROMANS 5:15-16 (TLB)

Christ, who suffered for you, is your example. Follow in his steps: He never sinned, never told a lie, never answered back when insulted; when he suffered he did not threaten to get even; he left his case in the hands of God who always judges fairly. He personally carried the load of our sins in his own body when he died on the cross, so that we can be finished with sin and live a good life from now on. For his wounds have healed ours! 1 PETER 2:21b-24 (TLB)

If we confess our sins, he is faithful and just and will forgive us our sins and purify us from all unrighteousness. 1 JOHN 1:9

It is for freedom that Christ has set us free. Stand firm, then, and do not let yourselves be burdened again by a yoke of slavery.... You ... were called to be free. But do not use your freedom to indulge the sinful nature; rather, serve one another in love. GALATIANS 5:1, 13

Part Twelve

Praying for Neighbours, Community, and Leaders

I Neglected My Neighbour

My neighbour needed me today, but I was too busy, Lord. A million things to do. I didn't take time to listen to her needs. But, Lord, you always have time for me. Help me turn aside from the busyness of life for people you want me to give attention to. Whether they are next door, at the supermarket, at my workplace, or wherever our paths cross. Bless my neighbour today. Help me slow down and be more sensitive to others' needs. I ask in Jesus' name, Amen.

Divine Appointments

Father, thank you for the people you bring into my life—not by accident but by divine appointment! Help me respond to your leading in how to pray for the friends, neighbours, and co-workers you've given me. Thank you for the opportunity to be a "Good Samaritan" in bringing them to you. May I not be deterred by the cost. Instead, let me rejoice in the rewards of having others come to know you personally. I'm so glad someone cared enough to share the Good News with me when I needed to know your love. Thank you, Lord. Amen.

Help Me with Sandpaper People

Heavenly Father, keep me tuned to you so I will know how to pray for the sandpaper people in my life. The ones who irritate me but who need your love. May I follow Jesus' example, who, when he was insulted, didn't answer back but left the judgment to you. That's hard to do, Lord. Please help me.

May I be willing to stand in prayer for those I associate with on a regular basis, as well as for strangers you bring across my path. Help me accept people as they are, Lord. To love them with your love. To see that they have potential because your mercy can redeem them. I ask in Jesus' name, Amen.

Prayer for My Pastor

Thank you, Lord, for our pastor. Bless ________ *(name)* with wisdom and understanding to guide our congregation in our present circumstances, and also for the future. Grant your strength to help our pastor stand firm in difficult times, without compromise. Keep him/her true to you, even though taking a stand for godly principles may bring criticism.

Bless our pastor's family, Lord. Because they fear you, may the angel of the Lord encamp around them and keep them safe. Give them a deep love for one another that will stand the test of time, even in the face of adversity.

I love our pastor(s), Lord, and thank you for the gift of his/her godly counsel. May your abundant blessings and favour rest upon Pastor ________ . In Jesus' name, Amen.

Prayer for Our Schools

Lord, I'm concerned about violence in our schools and the decline of moral values. Since you are no longer acknowledged in our school system, it's like a ship lost at sea. No direction … no point of reference. Oh, God, intervene in this situation. Put godly leaders in places of authority who can steer this ship in the way it should go. Give your favour and blessing to those policy-makers and teachers who are taking a stand against godlessness.

Lord, protect our children from the evils of gang violence, drug abuse, and promiscuity. Strengthen Christian young people to fearlessly share your truth with their peers. Lord, these children are the hope of our nation. Pour your love and grace into their lives. I pray in Jesus' name, Amen.

Prayer for the Justice System

Thank you, Lord, for your Word, which declares that you are a God of justice. You are perfect, faithful, and upright, and you do no wrong (Deuteronomy 32:4). Lord, I pray your divine justice will infiltrate the courts of our nation. You see the corruption and bribery that sometimes causes the innocent to suffer and the guilty to avoid judgment. I pray you will remove from office those who distort justice and deal treacherously with the innocent. Lord, I ask your forgiveness for the sins of our nation that have paved the way for injustice to rule. God, may your righteousness prevail. I ask in Jesus' name, Amen.

Prayer for Leaders

Lord, I pray our government leaders will acknowledge you as they make decisions that affect the people of our community and our nation. Help them resolve the issues concerning the needy and the poor. May they be humble and willing to serve the citizens of our area without favouritism. Help them refrain from dishonesty. Spare them from the corruption of greed and bribery. Lord, I ask that you give our leaders wise counsellors and godly wisdom. Thank you for pouring out your mercy upon our nation. Amen.

Scriptures for Our Nation's Leaders

He is the Rock, his works are perfect, and all his ways are just. A faithful God who does no wrong, upright and just is he. DEUTERONOMY 32:4

If the Lord delights in a man's way, he makes his steps firm; though he stumble, he will not fall, for the Lord upholds him with his hand.

PSALM 37:23-24

Make your face shine upon your servant and teach me your decrees. Streams of tears flow from my eyes, for your law is not obeyed. Righteous are you, O Lord, and your laws are right. The statutes you have laid down are righteous; they are fully trustworthy. PSALM 119:135-38

The Lord sustains the humble but casts the wicked to the ground. PSALM 147:6

Righteousness exalts a nation, but sin is a disgrace to any people. PROVERBS 14:34

The king's heart is in the hand of the Lord; he directs it like a watercourse wherever he pleases. PROVERBS 21:1

When the righteous thrive, the people rejoice; when the wicked rule, the people groan.... By justice a king gives a country stability, but one who is greedy for bribes tears it down.... If a king judges the poor with fairness, his throne will always be secure. PROVERBS 29:2, 4, 14

He who oppresses the poor shows contempt for their Maker, but whoever is kind to the needy honors God.... Righteousness exalts a nation, but sin is a disgrace to any people.

PROVERBS 14:31, 34

My hand has made both earth and skies, and they are mine. Yet I will look with pity on the man who has a humble and a contrite heart, who trembles at my word. ISAIAH 66:2 (TLB)

I urge, then, first of all, that requests, prayers, intercession and thanksgiving be made for everyone—for kings and all those in authority, that we may live peaceful and quiet lives in all godliness and holiness. This is good, and pleases God our Savior, who wants all men to be saved and to come to a knowledge of the truth.

1 TIMOTHY 2:1-4

Bibliography

Quin Sherrer and Ruthanne Garlock. *A Woman's Guide to Breaking Bondages* (Servant, Ann Arbor, Mich.: 1994).

Quin Sherrer and Ruthanne Garlock. *A Woman's Guide to Spirit-Filled Living* (Servant, Ann Arbor, Mich.: 1996).

Quin Sherrer and Ruthanne Garlock. *A Woman's Guide to Spiritual Warfare* (Servant, Ann Arbor, Mich.: 1991).

Quin Sherrer and Ruthanne Garlock. *The Spiritual Warrior's Prayer Guide* (Servant, Ann Arbor, Mich.: 1992).

Quin Sherrer and Ruthanne Garlock. *How to Pray for Your Family and Friends* (Servant, Ann Arbor, Mich.: 1990).

Quin Sherrer with Ruthanne Garlock. *How to Forgive Your Children* (Lynnwood, Wash.: Aglow, 1989).

Quin Sherrer. *How to Pray for Your Children* (Lynnwood, Wash.: Aglow, 1986).